Sheeply Horned Witch Romi

YOICHI ABE

1

CONTENTS

SLIDE
SAME HERE, HUH?
VRZZ
Sawada
Decline
Accept
VRZZ
!
SAWA-DA!
YOU OKAY?
WHERE ARE Y--
THE ROOF?
CHAK

THERE YOU ARE...
SENPAI.
OH.
Episode 1: White Earth
THEY'RE EVERY-WHERE.
There's a ton of 'em up here.
AND, LIKE, THESE SHEEP...
Baa
Baa
Baa
Baa
Baa
EVERY-ONE'S, LIKE, DEAD ASLEEP.
HEY, YOU PEEP THE REST OF THE SCHOOL?

WHAT IN THE HECK'S GOING ON?
SEN-PAI...
WHAT *ARE* YOU ON ABOUT?
Baa Baa
IF THERE'RE SHEEP AND SLEEPING PEOPLE EVERYWHERE, THEN OBVIOUSLY...
Pffft...
THESE SHEEP THAT'VE APPEARED AROUND THE WORLD EN MASSE...
HAVE PUT EVERYONE TO SLEEP!
Baa
Baa
Baa
Baa
UHH... WHAT? YOU OKAY THERE?
YA KNOW, LIKE...
ONE SHEEP, TWO SHEEP...
Baa
OKAY, HERE.
WATCH THIS.
Hop
ONE SHEEP...
TUMP!
......

TWO SHEEP...
HOP
TMP
UGH.
SHE'S DEFINITELY MESSING WITH ME AGAIN.
THREE SHEEP...
DOES SHE SERIOUSLY THINK THIS IS GONNA PUT ME TO SLEEP?
HOP
TMP
TEN SECONDS LATER...
SEVEN SHEEP...
WAVER...
EIGHT SHEEP...
WAVER...
GAAH! I'M SO SLEEPY!
NO WAY... DOES THIS MEAN... SHE'S RIGHT?
Baa
fluff
Baa
fluff

THIS MAY BE A STUPID QUESTION...
BUT WHY ARE WE THE ONLY ONES NOT SLEEPING?
AIN'T THAT WEIRD?
YOU *WERE* ASLEEP.
I REMOVED THE SPELL AND WOKE YOU UP.
WHAT?

DID YOU JUST SAY "SPELL"?
HUH?
WAIT, COME TO THINK OF IT...
WHEN I CAME TO, I WAS AT THE SCHOOL'S ENTRANCE.
I CAN'T REMEMBER ANYTHING BEFORE THEN.
LOOK... I MADE A WISH...
FOR EVERYONE BUT ME TO JUST DISAPPEAR.
AND THIS WAS THE RESULT.
GUESS THAT'S PART OF MY POWER NOW.
AND, WELL...
I HAD LOADS OF FUN BY MYSELF FOR A WHILE, BUT GOT SUPER BORED.
SO...

I WOKE YOU UP TO MESS WITH YOU.
MESS WITH ME, HUH?
Why not play with me instead?
LOOM
WHA--?
THAT'S THE PART THAT THROWS YOU?
!

TUG
TUG
WHETHER I'M MESSING WITH YOU OR PLAYING WITH YOU...
WE'RE STILL TOGETHER.
AFTER ALL...
STREEETCH...
YOU'RE MY TOY, SENPAI.
BIYOOON
......

Pf
ft!
Aha
ha
OH GOSH, YOUR CHEEKS!
THEY'RE *SOOO* STRETCHY!
Quit it!
THROB
THROB
THAT'S CUZ YOU KEEP STRETCHING 'EM!!
I SO LOVE MESSING WITH YOU.
TP
TP
HEY, SENPAI...

THE EARTH IS OURS UNTIL THE END!
WE'RE GOING TO HAVE SO MUCH FUN!

Episode 1: White Earth | End

Episode 2: Sawada's Horns

MY KOUHAI, SAWADA, TURNED INTO A SHEEP WITCH.
SO SHE'S GOT SHEEP HORNS ON HER HEAD NOW.
BUT ARE THEY REAL?
I HAVE MY DOUBTS.
FWUP
SHWP
KSSH
KSSH
I BET THEY'RE JUST HORN-SHAPED HEAD-PHONES.

SMILE...
SHE'S ALWAYS PRANKING ME, SO NO DOUBT.
STARE......
WHAT'S UP, SENPAI?
SAWADA...
MIND IF I TOUCH YOUR HORNS?
OOH, I GET IT. YOU DON'T THINK THEY'RE REAL.
OKAY.
GO AHEAD AND TOUCH THEM.
BUT WHAT DO I GET IN RETURN?
IF THEY'RE REAL, YOU CAN HIT ME. HARD.
DEAL.

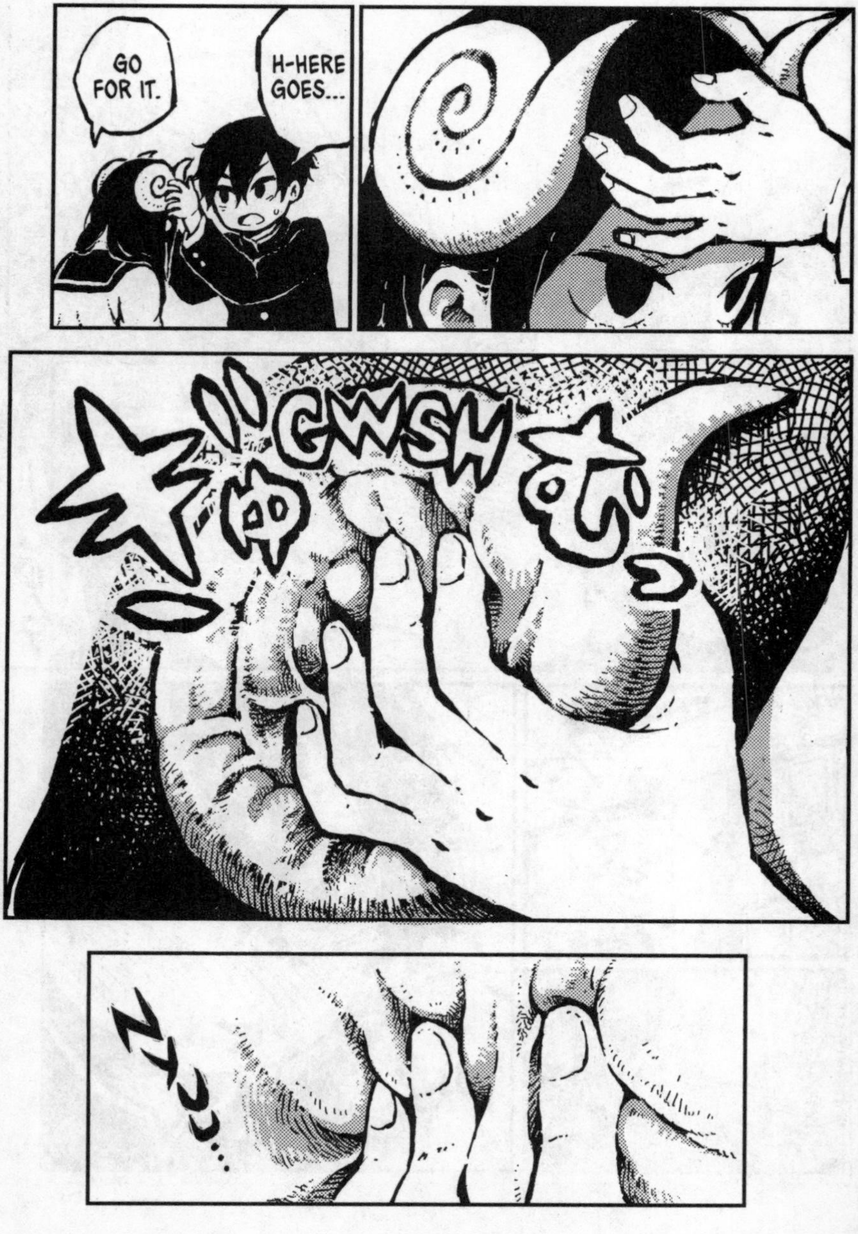
H-HERE GOES...
GO FOR IT.
CWSH
ZZZ...

MM...
JOLT
AH!
BA-KRSH!!

BUT...
OR JUST GO OFF...
WHEN I'M MESSING WITH YOU.
BTNK
I MEAN, SOME-TIMES I LIE...
TURNING INTO A WITCH...
Shp
AND PUTTING HUMANKIND TO SLEEP WITH MAGIC...
AND THE HORNS! TOTALLY TRUE AND SO REAL!
ER... SORRY FOR DOUBTING YOU.
Sip
BUT...
WHAT REALLY SURPRISED ME...
YEAH, THOSE HORNS...
DEFINITELY FELT LIKE THEY GREW OUT OF HER HEAD.
WAS THEIR TEXTURE.
NYUU...

THEY WERE SO, SO SOFT.
Sip
PAH!
BY THE WAY...
DID YOU ENJOY FEELING THEM UP?
TP TP
BA-DMP
HUH?!
WH-WH-WHAT?!
Fluster
Fluster
I-I-I--! WHADDYA MEAN?!
THEY'RE PRETTY SOFT, NO?
UH... Y-YEAH.
LIKE...THEY WEREN'T THE HARD HORNS THAT I WAS EXPECTING.
THEY'VE GOT A SKIN-LIKE TEXTURE, LIKE THEY WERE A PART OF YOUR BODY...
TRUE FACTS, SAME AS I THOUGHT.

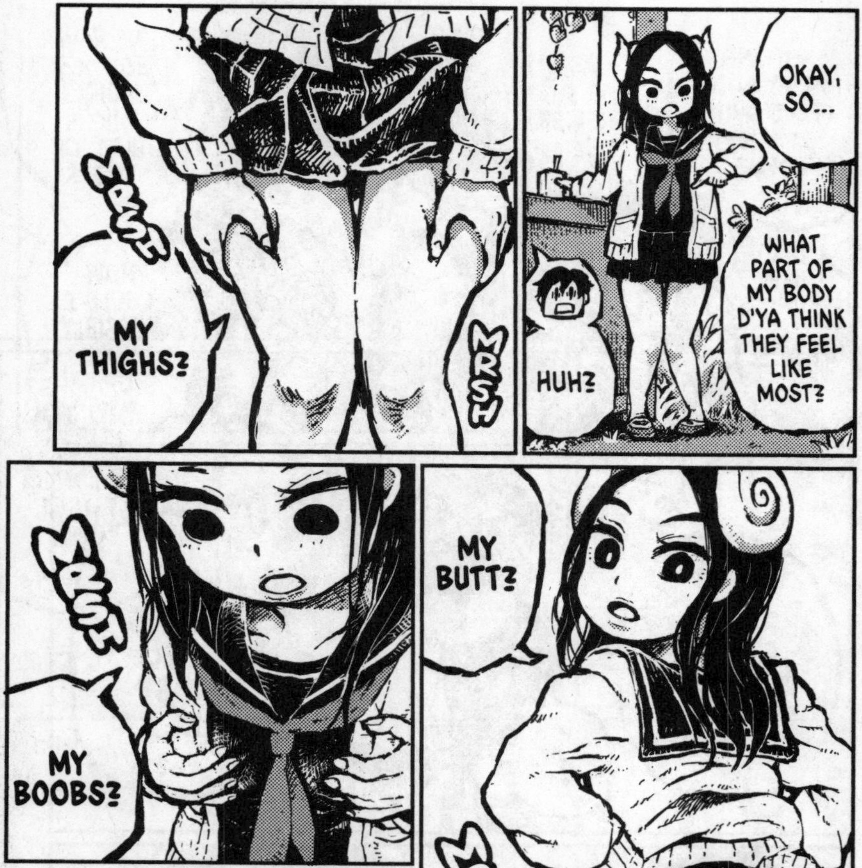
OKAY, SO...
WHAT PART OF MY BODY D'YA THINK THEY FEEL LIKE MOST?
HUH?
MRSH
MY THIGHS?
MRST
MY BUTT?
MRST
OR MAYBE...
MRST
MY BOOBS?
WHAT DO YOU THINK, SENPAI?
I...
WHY'RE YOU ASKING ME?!

I'VE NEVER TOUCHED A GIRL'S THIGHS, BUTT, OR BOOBS!
HOW COULD I POSSIBLY KNOW?! STOP IT!!
BLOOSH
CLENCH
HEE HEE HEE!
I FORGOT HOW LACKING YOU WERE IN THAT DEPART-MENT, HA HA! (JK!)
AS FOR THE ANSWER ...
NOTHING ON MY BODY FEELS QUITE LIKE MY HORNS.
WHAT?!
STRETCH
MY HORNS FEEL MOST LIKE...
YOUR CHEEKS, SENPAI.
!
YUP.
MWSH
MWSH
THAT CON-FIRMS IT.
TRY TOUCHING BOTH AGAIN.
MWSH
MWSH

MWSH
MWSH
MWSH
MWSH
MWSH
MWSH
MWSH
MWSH
MWSH
MWSH
MWSH
MWSH
MWSH
MWSH
MWSH
MWSH
YOU'RE ...
YOU'RE RIGHT! THEY'RE ALMOST THE EXACT SAME!

TOLD YOU SO!
GOSH! TO THINK, I HAVE SOMETHING THAT FEELS AS AMAZING AS YOUR CHEEKS...
ON MY VERY OWN BODY!
I'M SO HAPPY I MIGHT PEE MYSELF!
MY HORNS CAN'T STRETCH LIKE YOUR CHEEKS THOUGH, SO YOU STILL WIN.
THAT MEANS ...
MWSH
I CAN BASICALLY FEEL HER HORNS WHENEVER I WANT.

Episode 2: Sawada's Horns | End

Episode 3: Panties and Othello

HERE'S THE GAME, SENPAI.
SKRIKA
SKRIKA
THE FIRST ONE TO HIT AN OBSTACLE LOSES.
SKRIKA
SKRIKA

WHOA?!
S-SAWADA...!!
SHE'S GOT NO UNDER-WEAR!!
WHAT'S WITH YOU HIGH SCHOOL GIRLS?!!
OH, THAT!
I TOOK ALL THEIR UNDERWEAR OFF.
BA-THMP
AHA!
YOU LOSE!
WH-WHY'D YOU DO SOME-THING LIKE THAT?!!
WHY...?
SO THAT I'D HAVE PLENTY OF SPARE CHANGES, OBVIOUSLY.
shwf
shwf
I ONLY HAD THE PAIR I WAS WEARING, AFTER ALL.

BUT PANTIES, *WEEELL*... YOU KNOW.
NOT HAVING A BRA DOESN'T BUG ME...
SO I'D BE WITHOUT PANTIES FOR A DAY WHEN I WASHED THEM.
fwp fwp
TAK
THIS WHOLE TIME?
WAIT, SO YOU'VE BEEN LIVING AT SCHOOL...
RIGHT.
SO...
I TOOK THE FIFTY OR SO PAIRS I GRABBED...
AND WASHED AND DRIED THEM ALL.
VWUM
VWUM

BUT IN THE END, I BURNED THEM WITHOUT WEARING A SINGLE PAIR.
KTAK
WELL, I MEAN...
FWP FWP
HUH?!
WH- WHY?!
BURNED 'EM, HUH? GOTCHA...
WAIT, WHAT?
GWOOOAR
THINK ABOUT IT. KINDA GROSS TO WEAR SOME STRANGER'S UNDERWEAR, RIGHT?
SO I BURNED THEM ALL!
KRAKL...
KRAKL...

UMM... I THINK I WORE THEM YESTER-DAY...
AND WASHED THEM THIS MORNING.
UH... WAIT, SO RIGHT NOW...
AND NOW I LIVE IN JUST THIS ONE PAIR.
...
SO I'M COM-MANDO RIGHT NOW!

WANT TO SEE MY HAND-STAND?
ST-STOOOP!!
I WAS KIDDING...
SENPAI.
OF COURSE I'M WEARING PANTIES.
SHWF
GRAB
HEY!
STOP THAT!!
WHY'RE YOU SHOWING ME?!!
GRIP
HUH?
IT'S FINE. YOU SAW--I'M WEARING THEM.

THAT'S BESIDE THE POINT!
YOU CAN'T JUST GO AROUND FLASHING PEOPLE!!
BLUSH
OKAY, OKAY.
OH!
BUT...
I REALLY DID BURN THOSE OTHER PANTIES, THOUGH.
THESE ONES ARE BRAND-NEW.
I MADE THEM WITH MAGIC.
FWIP
NO WAY AM I WALKING AROUND IN A DIRTY PAIR.
GAAAH!! I DON'T NEED TO SEE 'EM!!
I REALIZED THAT, RATHER THAN STEALING OTHER GIRLS' PANTIES...
I COULD JUST MAKE SOME WITH WOOL!
VRRR VRRR VRRR VRRR
Shave the sheep.
Take that!
MAGIIIC~~~
Use magic on the wool!!
BIBBIDI-SKIVVIDI-EWE!
100% wool!!
Panties!!

OH! DON'T WORRY, I MADE SOME FOR YOU, TOO.
TAK
HUH? SO...I'LL BE LIVING HERE, TOO?
HMM... I GUESS MY FAMILY'LL BE DEEP ASLEEP.
SO THIS IS FINE.
WOO-HOO!
I WIN!
SEN-PAI...
ARE YOU FEELING HUNGRY YET?
YEAH, A LITTLE BIT.
WHAT'RE WE HAVING?
SALTED ONIGIRI.
HA HA!
YOU'RE A BIG FAN, EH?

Episode 3: Panties and Othello | End

FSS
SHHH
SHHH
HHHH

Episode 4: Salted Onigiri and Monsters

MMM
...
SMELLS
SO
GOOD...

YOU REALLY THINK WE CAN EAT...
THIS MANY?
PRESS
PRESS
lick
I NEED AT *LEAST* THIS MANY.
OTHERWISE, I CAN'T MAINTAIN THE BARRIER.
BARRIER?
WHAT BARRIER?
om
om
YOU SEE...
THERE'S THIS BLACK MIASMA DRIFTING OUTSIDE THE SCHOOL.
omf
NOM
NOM
NOM

IT GETS THICKER BY THE DAY...
SLOWLY ENCROACHING ON OUR LITTLE WORLD HERE.
UHH, THAT SOUNDS PRETTY BAD.
om om
YEAH, SURE, I GUESS SO.
ESPECIALLY WHEN YOU CONSIDER...
NOM
IT'S PUMPING OUT MONSTERS...
NOM
NOM
ALMOST NON-STOP.
NOM
NOM
JOLT
WHA...? M-MONSTERS?
THAT'S WHAT THE BARRIER IS FOR.
KEEPING THE MONSTERS OUT OF HERE.
TAKES A BIT OF TIME TO CONVERT INTO MAGICAL ENERGY, SO DO YOU WANT TO TAKE A LOOK?
URP!
A-AT WHAT ...?
THE MONSTERS.

CAN WE STOP BY THE RICE SHOP UP AHEAD?
OUR STOCK IS RUNNING LOW, SO WE NEED TO GET MORE.
GOTCHA.
米 店
RICE SHOP
SENPAI.
COULD YOU PUT ANOTHER TALLY MARK THERE?
WOW.
SHE'S ACTUALLY BEEN LEAVING MONEY...
WHENEVER SHE TAKES SOME RICE.
SHE'S PRETTY THOUGHTFUL...
WITH THINGS LIKE THAT.

THAT MONEY WAS "DONATED" BY CLASSMATES I HATE, *HEH HEH HEH!*
WHAT ?!!
I SHOULD'VE KNOWN BETTER.
MAN...
IT'S SO QUIET...
WITHOUT ALL THE PEOPLE AROUND.
IN A WAY, IT'S ACTUALLY PRETTY RELAXING.
OH!!
SENPAI, THIS WAY.

LOOKS SORTA LIKE THE OCEAN.
THE MIASMA DOES THAT.
SEE THAT OVER THERE?
HM?
AND THERE'RE PROBABLY MONSTERS HIDING OUT THERE.
PLEASE GO TAKE A LOOK.
WHAT?!
......
PLEASE. GO. TAKE. A. LOOK!
peek...
A-AM I GONNA GET ATTACKED?
I DON'T KNOW.
WHA~?

SHEFF...
DOESN'T SEEM TO BE ANY...
PLAP...
PLAP...
PLAP...
PLAP...
PLAP...
PLAP...
AH. THERE IT IS.
GLANCE...

PLAP...
AH...
DASH
UWAH—!!

GRSH
GRSH
GRSH
WHAT THE--?!
THEY'RE ALL OVER THE PLACE!!
H-HUH?!
SAWADA?!
THERE SHE IS!!
SHE RAN BACK WITHOUT ME!!
SEN-PAI!!
YOU BEST START RUNNING!!
THE SCHOOL GROUNDS ARE THE SAFE ZOOONE!!
Pfft
DAMN IT!! DON'T MAKE FUN OF MY PANIC!!
BA-TAM
!

THAT'S WHAT THE BARRIER DOES. PFFFT!
I THINK YOU CAN SEE HOW DANGEROUS IT IS...
Keh heh heh! "Uwah!!" So funny...
SO PLEASE TRY NOT TO GO OUT THERE. BFFFT!
Huff!
Huff!
IS SHE SERIOUSLY STILL LAUGHING AT ME?
GWUUUUR
!
AH.
I'M ALMOST DONE... DIGESTING...
Huff!
Huff!
GWUUUUR
GWUUUR
HNN!!
Huff!
Huff!
I-I'M COOL. MY GUTS ARE CHURNING LIKE CRAZY...
AND IT KINDA HURTS ...
GWUUUUR
GWUUUR
HEY!
YOU OKAY?! WHAT'S WRONG?!

HNGH...
SQUEEZE
......
GUH!
GUHN!
HNN!
HERE IT...
COMES ...
OH NO...
JOLT
BAHHH!
HNGH!

SHU
SHU
SO, THE RICE I EAT AND DIGEST...
TURNS INTO WHITE MIASMA AND IS RELEASED BY THE SHEEP.
WHOA!!
THE HECK IS GOING ON?!!
IT'S MAKING WHITE MIASMA.
I LINKED MY BOWELS TO THE SHEEP AROUND THE SCHOOL WITH MAGIC.

SO THE BLACK MIASMA SHOULDN'T HAVE ANY IMPACT ON US!
IT STRENGTH-ENS...
MY BARRIER SIGNIFICANTLY.
WAIT, IF THIS SMOKE'S A BYPRODUCT OF HER DIGESTIVE SYSTEM...
HUNH. COME TO THINK OF IT...
I'M BASICALLY LETTING LOOSE FARTS.
SHE ACTUALLY SAID IT!!
YOU'RE PROTECTED BY MY FARTS...

SENPAI, YOU'RE SUR-ROUNDED...
BY MY BIG RIPPED FARTS.
LIVING A PEACEFUL EXISTENCE ...
PROTECTED BY MY FARTS.
Paff
COULDJA QUIT IT WITH THE FART STUFF?!
I GOT IT THE FIRST TIME!
HEE HEE!
SHE'S HAVING WAY TOO MUCH FUN BUGGING ME.
PROTECTED BY YOUR KOUHAI'S FARTS... PFFFT!
STILL NOT DONE...
SHUOOOO...

Episode 4: Salted Onigiri and Monsters | End

WHAT ARE YOU DRAWING?

Episode 5: The Warm Pool

OOH!
THAT'S THE MONSTER FROM EARLIER!
YOUR SKILL NEVER CEASES TO IMPRESS ME.
HUH? YOU'VE LOOKED AT MY DRAWINGS BEFORE?
OH, YES. MANY TIMES.
I-I SEE...

Y'KNOW, HON-ESTLY...
MY HEAD'S FEELIN' KINDA LIKE THIS MIASMA.
ALL HAZY 'N' STUFF.
LIKE, MY MEMORIES FEEL SORTA FUZZY.
I'VE GOT THIS NAGGING SENSE I'M FORGETTING SOMETHING SUPER IMPOR-TANT...
I CAN'T EXPLAIN THIS FEELING...
......
IT'S LATE.
HOW ABOUT WE GET WASHED UP AND CALL IT A DAY?
SENPAI.

CLEAN UP...
IN THE SCHOOL'S POOL?
PWAAAAAAAA
PLOSH
JWSSH
I USED MAGIC TO MAKE THE WATER NICE AND HOT. IT'S PERFECT!
SO...
LET'S HOP IN, SENPAI!
WHAT ?!
T-TO-GETHER?!! N-NO... NO WAY!!
STEAM
STEAM

SHWEF
3
UWAGH!
OH...A SWIM-SUIT?
SMILE...
DID YOU REALLY THINK I'D BATHE WITH YOU NAKED...
SENPAI?
PLOOSH
NOT A CHAA-ANCE!
NUH-UH!
SUCH A PAIN.
THAT THING YOU WERE SAYING ABOUT FUZZY MEMORIES...
plsh plsh
IT'S A SIDE EFFECT OF ME FORCING YOU AWAKE.
SO, UM...
SORRY ABOUT THAT.

WHAT?
WHY'RE YOU APOLOGIZING?!
SERIOUSLY, I DON'T CARE.
HONESTLY, I APPRECIATE YOU WAKING ME UP.
THE OLD WORLD WAS SO NOISY I COULD BARELY TAKE IT.
Y'SEE, I'M REALLY NOT GOOD WITH LARGE CROWDS OR LOTS OF NOISE.
THIS NEW WORLD YOU MADE IS COMFORTING.
blush
LIKE, THE MONSTERS SHOCKED ME AT FIRST...
BUT THEY WERE PRETTY EXCITING, TOO!
SO MUCH SO I ALMOST WISH WE COULD EXPLORE OUTSIDE...
AND SEE *MORE* MONSTERS.

I'M DONE BATHING, I THINK.
ZA-PLSH...
......
UH... DID I SAY SOME-THING WEIRD?
O-OKAY...
PLSH

Episode 5: The Warm Pool | End

Episode 6: Naked at School

MMM... I SLEPT SO WELL!
Stretch
stretch
SEEMS LIKE SHE'S BACK TO NORMAL.
PHEW...
THIS WOOL IS SO SOFT AND FLUFFY.
MAKES FOR A GREAT BED! HNNNN!

STRETCH
WHAT WAS UP WITH...
THAT LOOK SHE HAD AT THE POOL?
!
LEAN
TP TP TP TP
WHAT'S UP?
HOW ABOUT WE WORK ON CLEANING THE SCHOOL UP?
fwp
HEY, SENPAI ...

LET'S CLEAR OUT ALL THESE SLUMBERING EYESORES!
THEY'RE IN THE WAY.
WE'LL STUFF 'EM IN THE GYM FOR NOW.
Hnph.
THERE'S NO WAY!
YOU WANNA CARRY ALL THESE PEOPLE BY OURSELVES?
NOT TO WORRY.
GRAB
GRAB
I MAGICKED SOME OF THE SHEEP TO WALK ON TWO LEGS!
DUN
WE'LL BE DONE MOVING EVERYONE IN NO TIME!

ALL RIGHT!
THAT'S ALL OF THEM!
YEAH, IT'S WAY BETTER LIKE THIS.
HEY, SAWA--
HUH?
WHERE'D SHE GO?
HEEEY!
ON THE THIRD FLOOR, *SENPAAAI!*

THE HECK ARE YOU DOING UP THERE?
NOW THAT THE SCHOOL'S ALL CLEAN, WEREN'T YOU GONNA DO SOMETHING?
HERE, TAKE THESE.
shwp
Fwap
WHAT'D YOU JUST DROP?
THE PANTIES I JUST TOOK OFF.
WAIT THERE A MOMENT, PLEASE.
WHAAAAT?!!
H- HEY! WHAT'RE YOU...
D- DOING?!

I TOOK OFF ALL MY CLOTHES, SO I'M FULLY IN THE BUFF UP HERE.
WH-WHAT THE HECK?!!
SAWA-WA-WA-WA-WAAA!!
TAKE OFF YOUR CLOTHES TOO, PLEASE.
HUH?
YOU GET NAKED DOWN THERE, AND DON'T YOU DARE COME UP HERE, NO MATTER WHAT.
AND LIKE, I PROMISE NOT TO GO DOWN TO YOU.
3
SEN-PAAAI!
2
WHA-AAT?
IT'S A FUN GAME WHERE WE BARE OURSELVES WHILE BARE.
WHAT DO YOU THINK?
DOESN'T THE IDEA GET YOUR HEART RACING?
I MEAN...I GUESS SO? BUT STILL...
THEN LET'S GET TO IT!
HOLD IT! I DIDN'T AGREE TO ANY-THING!

DON'T YOU THINK IT'S A BIT UNFAIR...
FOR ME TO BE THE ONLY ONE WHO'S NAKED?
WHAT'S UNFAIR IS YOU TAKING YOUR CLOTHES OFF OUTTA NO-WHERE!!
SENPAI, DO YOU THINK THERE'S SOMETHING SPECIAL ABOUT YOUR NAKED BODY?
BECAUSE THERE ISN'T!
WHY ARE YOU ASSUMING PEOPLE *WANT* TO SEE THAT, *HM?*
BESIDES, THERE'S NO ONE HERE! SUCH LOW SELF-ES--
FINE, FINE, JUST STOP.
WHAT THE HECK AM I DOING?
SENPAIII!
ARE YOU NAKED *YEEET?*
YES, I AM!

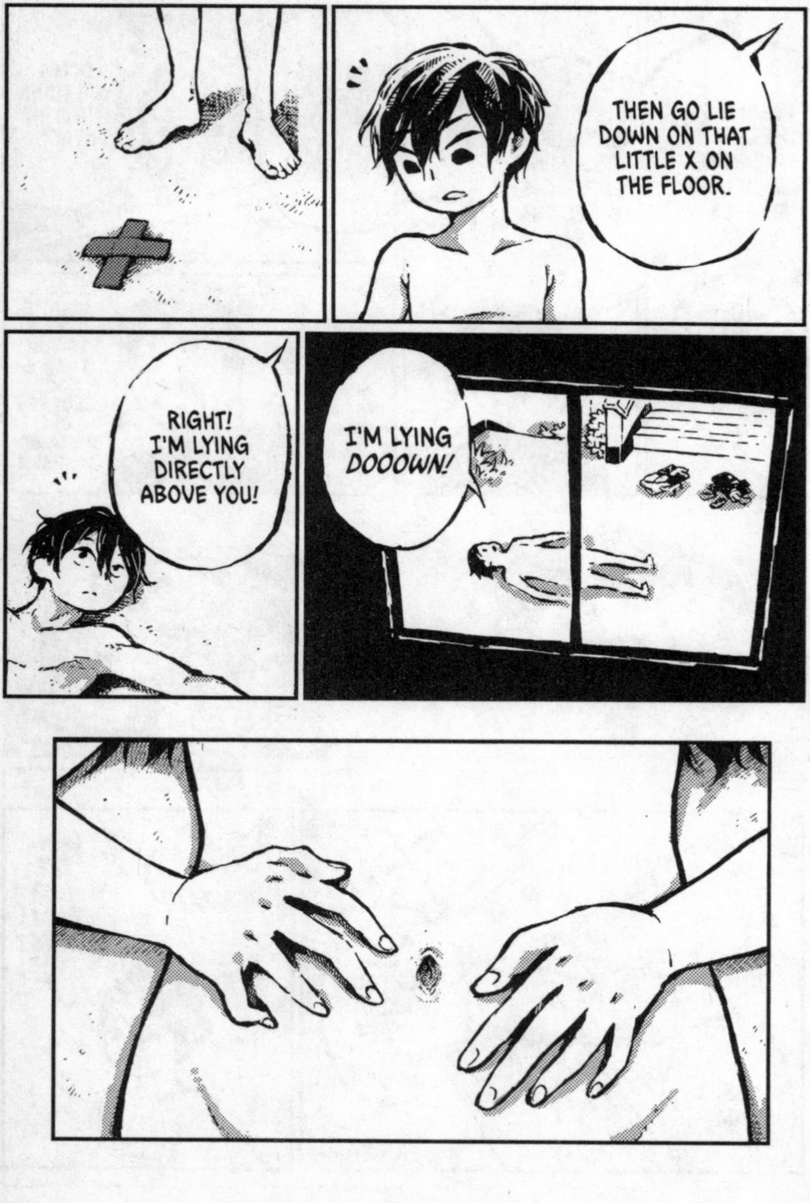
THEN GO LIE DOWN ON THAT LITTLE X ON THE FLOOR.
RIGHT! I'M LYING DIRECTLY ABOVE YOU!
I'M LYING *DOOOWN!*

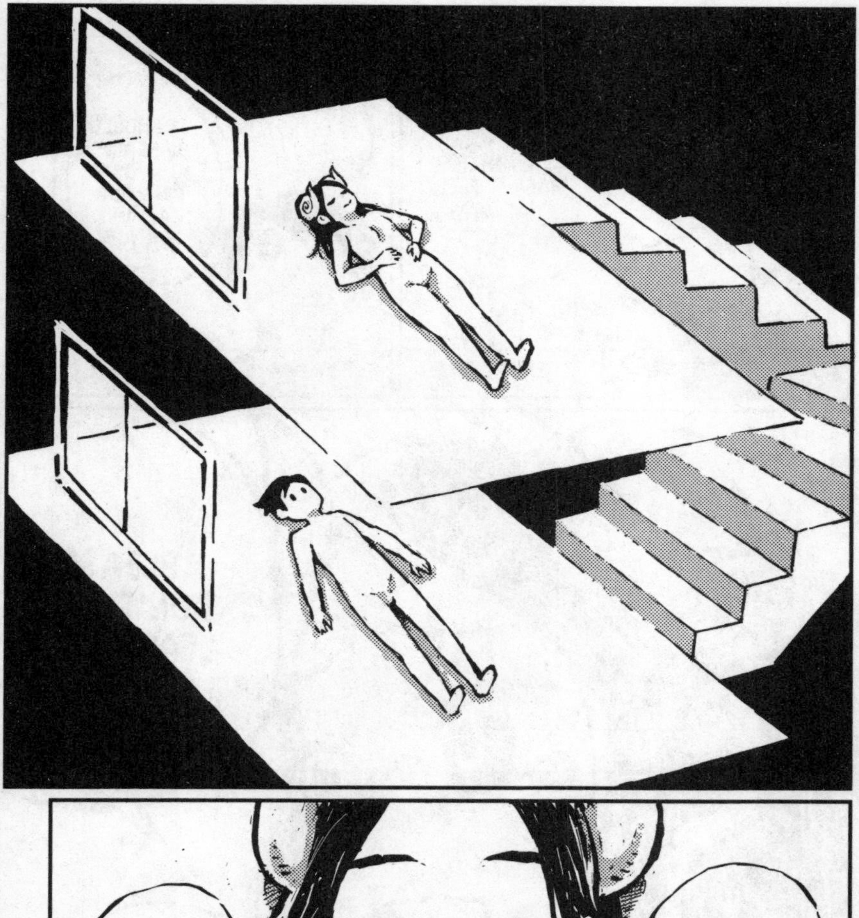
SO IF THE SCHOOL BUILDING IS BASICALLY MY BODY...
THAT MEANS YOU'RE INSIDE MY WOMB RIGHT NOW.

SO...
EVEN IF IT'S NOT, I WANT TO MAKE IT FEEL THAT WAY!
......
IT SHOULD BE REALLY COMFORT-ABLE AND CALMING FOR YOU.
PLEASE DON'T EVER LEAVE ME...
SENPAI.

"LIKE, THE MONSTERS SHOCKED ME AT FIRST, BUT THEY WERE PRETTY EXCITING, TOO! SO MUCH SO I ALMOST WISH WE COULD EXPLORE OUTSIDE AND SEE MORE MONSTERS."
OH...
NO, NO!
THAT'S NOT WHAT I--
I KNOW.
TP TP
I KNOW YOU DON'T ACTUALLY WANT TO LEAVE HERE.
I CAN TELL THAT MUCH.
I KNOW YOU'RE COMFORTABLE.
SO I'M SORRY ABOUT THIS LITTLE JOKE.
PLEASE, JUST FORGET IT HAPPENED.
I GOT A LITTLE BIT SCARED IS ALL.
SAWADA...
I... AM WELL AWARE OF HOW CURIOUS YOU ARE, SENPAI.

I MADE THIS WORLD SO THAT THE TWO OF US...
COULD BE COMFORTABLE.
AND YET, I STILL TRIED TO LOCK YOU AWAY.
I'M REALLY SORRY.
......
PWOP
SO, LET'S GO TOMORROW!
JONK
ACK!
AH!
G-GO WHERE?
fwp
EXPLORE BEYOND THE SCHOOL.

Episode 6: Naked at School | End

ARE YOU SERI-OUS?!
WITH YOU BEHIND THE WHEEL?!
CAN YOU EVEN DRIVE?!!
WHAT?!
WE'RE TAKING A TRUCK?!

Episode 7: Monster Field Guide

I KNOW I ASKED YOU LAST NIGHT...
BUT I WANT TO MAKE DOUBLY SURE.
LOOK AT ME GO!
VRRRRRM
HALT
HEY, SENPAI.
I CAN DRIVE USING MAGIC!
See? No hands or feet!
DOESN'T MATTER IF I KNOW HOW TO DRIVE OR NOT!
W-WOW. MAGIC SURE IS HANDY, HUH?

WHEN I LOOKED OUT FROM THE SCHOOL ROOF YESTERDAY MORNING...
ALMOST EVERYTHING NEARBY HAD BEEN CONSUMED BY THE BLACK MIASMA.
SO IT'LL LIKELY BE FAR DIFFERENT COMPARED TO WHEN WE SET OUT THE OTHER DAY.
WE CAN EXPECT MORE MONSTERS AS WELL.

SO...ARE YOU SURE ABOUT THIS?
SURE AM!
IF THERE'S NEW SPECIES OUT THERE, I WANNA PEN A FIELD GUIDE!
A MONSTER FIELD GUIDE!
......
GLAD TO SEE SOMEONE IS AT EASE.

WELL ...
THEY'RE NOT ALL THAT FERO- CIOUS, SO I'M SURE WE'LL BE FINE.
OKAY...
OFF WE GO!

Episode 7: Monster Field Guide | End

WOW...
MOST OF IT REALLY HAS BEEN CONSUMED.
OH!
CAN WE STOP HERE?
SURE.
SKR
BLSH PLSH PLSH
I WANNA TAKE MY TIME WALKING AROUND...
AND ENJOY THE VIEW AS WE EXPLORE.

Episode 8: Location Exploration

OOH, VERY NICE. BEST SKETCH THE SCENERY, TOO!
AH!
THERE'S THOSE SAME MONSTERS!
Skritch Skritch
HWAH ?!!
MORE AND MORE ARE GATHERING.
AH.
Skritch
Skritch
WELL, AS LONG AS YOU STAY NEAR ME OR MY SHEEP, WE SHOULD BE COOL.
BUT THE LONGER WE STAY, THE MORE DANGEROUS IT'LL BECOME.
R-RIGHT ...
FORGET THE SKETCHES.
I'LL TAKE PICS WITH MY PHONE AND DRAW THEM LATER.
KA-SNAP
KA-SNAP

KA-SNAP
IF THOSE GUYS WERE IN A FANTASY BOOK...
THEY'D PROB-ABLY BE GOBLINS.
HEE HEE!
YEAH.
THROOM THROOM
THROOM
THROOM
HM?
WHAT'S THAT SOUND?

ZSHHA A
THROOM THROOM
KA-SNAP SNAP SNAP
KA-SNAP SNAP SNAP
AND ...
AND THAT THING!!
IT'S A DRAGON!! RIGHT?! RIGHT?!!
GOTTA BE!!

YEAH! ♡

OKAY.
LET'S GO EXPLORE A BIT FARTHER OUT.
SURE!

VRROOOON

Episode 8:
Location Exploration | End

Episode 9: Re-Dyeing

OOH...
glup
glup
AND THIS IS...
A SLIME, HUH?
KA-SNAP
prod
prod
SHLUP
SHUAWU
AAAA
IT JUST...
DIS-SOLVED...

I-IT DIS-SOLVED OUR CLOTHES ...
BUT NOT OUR BODIES...
ZUNOZO...
SHUWAAAAA
STARE~~.....!! GRRR~~...!!
YOU ALL GOOD, SAWADA?
squilp
squilp

IT DIDN'T GET MY UNDERWEAR, SO I'M FINE.
YOU'RE ONE TO TALK, MR. BIRTHDAY SUIT.
SHUT UP! AND DON'T LOOK AT MEEE!!
THAT'S DEFINITELY NOT FINE!!
I REALLY DON'T MIND IF YOU STAY NAKED.
stare... stare... staaare...
PLEASE, HAVE MERCY!
DO SOMETHING ABOUT THIS!
HEEEY, SHEEPIES!
fwip
fwip
SHWP
VWRRRRRRRR
?
?

THERE WE GO! IMPROVISED WOOL CLOTHING!
THIS WILL DO FOR NOW.
GLAD I'M NOT NAKED ANYMORE.
fwp
BUT SORRY ...
AND THANKS, SHEEPIES.
UM, SENPAI ...
I'M REALLY SORRY. YOU PROTECTED ME...
crumple...
AND YOUR PHONE PAID THE PRICE.
I CAN FIX IT WITH MAGIC...
BUT THE DATA...
NO WORRIES! I GOT A GOOD LOOK AT EVERYTHING...
SO I'LL GO OFF MY BRAIN DATA!

AND FROM NOW ON...
I'LL LOOK EVEN CLOSER...
AND SEAR EVERY-THING INTO MY BRAIN!!
AAAHH!! SENPAI, DON'T LOOK TOO CLOSELY AT THAT THING!!
IT LOOKS LIKE A GORGON! YOU'LL BE TURNED TO STONE!!
WHA-AAT?!
plsh
plsh

WHOA!
A GOLEM!

GAAAH! I THOUGHT WE WERE DEAD FOR SURE!
I KNOOOW!
WOW! IT'S ALREADY GROWING BACK!
KRAKL
KRAKL

HEY, SENPAI...
nom
om
MONCH
MONCH
THANK YOU FOR PROTECTING ME EARLIER.
HUH?
OH, FROM THE SLIME?
MM-HMM.
IT MADE ME REALLY HAPPY.
W-WELL...
YOU THANKING ME AGAIN KINDA MAKES ME BLUSH.
fwip

DESPITE THE EFFORTS OF ME AND THE SHEEP, THE MONSTER POPULATION KEEPS GROWING.
ANY DAY NOW, THE NIGHTMARE WILL CONSUME EVERYTHING.
THE BLACK MIASMA GNAWING IN MY MIND IS THICKER THAN I THOUGHT.
I CAN'T CONTROL IT ANYMORE.
I BETTER ENJOY WHAT LITTLE TIME I HAVE...
LIVING HAPPY AND FULL ALONGSIDE SENPAI.

Episode 9: Re-Dyeing | End

Episode 10: Public Baths, the People Storage Area, and...

SENPAI, LOOK!
THAT MUST BE A SIREN, I GUESS?
YEAH!
OOH, KELPIES.

HUNH.
La la la la la la...
Public Bath
HOW ARE THE BATHS STILL RUNNING?

KRAKL
KRAKL
A SALA-MANDER'S BOILING THE WATER.
HERE'S THE CULPRIT.
GWOOOOO
OOOOAAAR
SENPAI!
MIGHT AS WELL TAKE ADVANTAGE, DON'T YOU THINK?
HN......

THIS IS SOOO NICE!
ME TOO!
HAAH... I SERIOUSLY NEEDED THIS.
AH.
THAT REMINDS ME.

WHERE'D ALL THE OTHER SLEEPING PEOPLE END UP?
LIKE WHEN WE WENT TO BUY RICE...
I EXPECTED TO SEE PEOPLE ALL OVER THE STREETS.
BUT I HAVEN'T SEEN A SOUL.
......
OH, SAME WITH YOUR SHEEP...
IS IT REALLY ALL THAT INTEREST-ING?
WELL, YEAH, KINDA...
za-plsh
UWAH!!
PWOP
SHALL WE GO HAVE A LOOK-SEE?
HUH?! L-LOOK AT WHAT?!
THE PEOPLE STORAGE AREA.

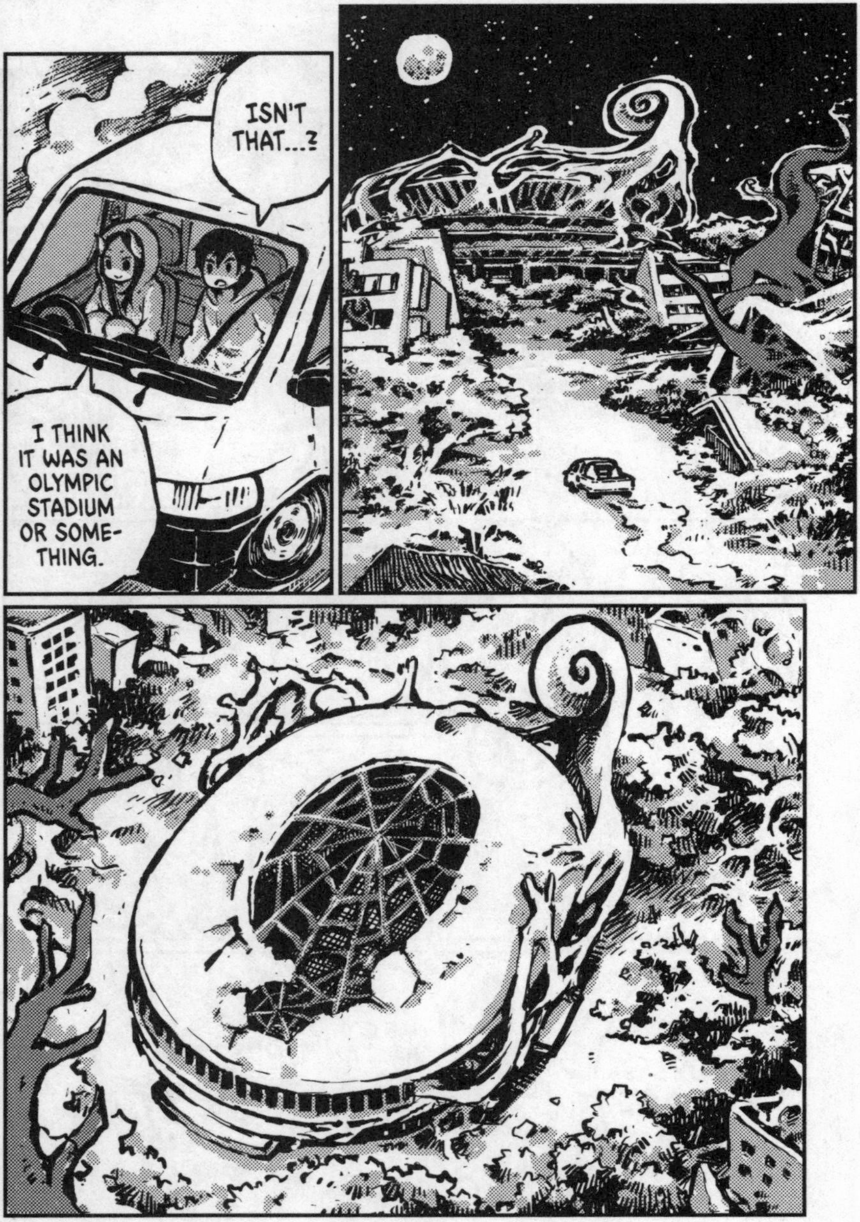
ISN'T THAT...?
I THINK IT WAS AN OLYMPIC STADIUM OR SOME-THING.

WH...
WHAT THE HECK IS THIS?
......
DID THE MONSTERS DO THIS?
FWOO
FWOO
WHY...?
WITH THE OLYMPICS ON HOLD, IT'S NOT LIKE IT WAS IN USE.
SO NOW IT'S A PEOPLE STORAGE AREA.
ARE THESE SPIDER-WEBS?

BECAUSE THEY WON'T ACCEPT THIS REALITY.
DON'T YOU THINK IT'S STRANGE...
THAT THINGS BORN FROM THE BLACK MIASMA WITHIN ME ARE THE "MONSTERS"?
I MADE THIS WORLD WHAT IT IS.
WHY AREN'T THE PEOPLE THAT I UTTERLY LOATHE THE *REAL* "MONSTERS"?

MONSTERS AROUND HERE ACT BASED ON HOW I THINK.
SAWA... DA?
UH...
ZA-THOOM
ZA-THOOM
WH...
WHAT'S GOING ON?!!
ZA-THOOM
ZA-THOOM
!!

DASH
DASH
A HUGE SPIDER!
IS TH-THAT AN ARACHNE?
LOOKS LIKE IT CAPTURED SOME MORE PEOPLE.
SHRUU!
OH?
SOME-THING FELL OFF.
Pyun

GRSH
GRSH
GRSH
PO—N
GN—K
ROLL
ROLL
ROLL
ROLL
ROLL
HALT
WAIT...
ISN'T THIS...

TAKADA, FROM THE CLASS BESIDE OURS?
HUH? WHAT'S SOMEBODY FROM SCHOOL DOING HERE?
......
FWIP
THAT WAS FASTER THAN I EXPECTED.
WHAT?
SHFF...

SENPAI...
THE SCHOOL... IT'S DEAD.
WHA ...?!
THE MONSTERS GOT THROUGH THE BARRIER AND DESTROYED THE BUILDING.
S-SAWADA ...
HUH?!
WH-WHAT DOES THAT MEAN?
WHAT?
THE SCHOOL'S DEAD?

HOW?!! I THOUGHT THAT WITH THE WHITE MIASMA...
THE MONSTERS COULDN'T GET IN!!
IT REACHED ITS LIMIT.
THE WORLD OUTSIDE THE SCHOOL HAS BEEN COMPLETELY CONSUMED BY THE BLACK MIASMA.
MY BARRIER COULD ONLY DO SO MUCH.
IT WAS ONLY A MATTER OF TIME.
......
LET'S GET GOING.
OKAY.
HUH?
WHERE?
WE'RE GOING TO TAKE ONE LAST LOOK AT THE SCHOOL'S CORPSE.
AND THERE'S SOMETHING I WANT TO GIVE YOU WHEN WE GET THERE.

Episode 10: Public Baths, the People Storage Area, and... | End

Episode 11

Recollection

HRMM...
THE DRAGON LOOKS FINE AS A SKETCH...
SHK
K
DUN
FLAP
FLAP
HFF!
THE SLIME'S DEAD!
SHFF
BUT INKING IT WILL BE A HUGE PAIN.
MAYBE I'LL GIVE UP ON THIS ONE.
Skrit
Skrit
NAH ...
AND IT'D BE BORING TO NOT PUBLISH THIS!
GOTTA DRAW LOTS IF I WANNA GET BETTER.

HEY, URYUU.
HEADED TO YOUR ONE-MAN MANGA CLUB?
WOULD YOU QUIT IT WITH THAT?
I TOLD YOU, IT'S NOT A ONE-MAN THING.
SHWP
MIGHT AS WELL BE, SEEING AS THE OTHER MEMBERS NEVER SHOW UP.
SURE, I GUESS SO...
SO WALK HOME WITH ME, DUDE! C'MON! I'M SO LONELY!
GOTTA FINISH MY PRELIM SKETCH WORK FIRST.
SEE YA.
THE MANGA CLUB'S ROOM IS WAAAY UP THE STAIRS...
AT THE TOP OF THE SCHOOL ...

FROM THE OUTSIDE, IT LOOKS LIKE THIS.
IN THIS LITTLE BUILDING ON THE ROOF.
FROM AN ISOMETRIC VIEW, IT LOOKS LIKE THIS.
THIS PART RIGHT HERE IS THE CLUB-ROOM.
Door to the Roof
AS MY BUD SAID, IT'S A ONE-MAN OPERATION, BUT THAT DOESN'T MEAN I'M ALWAYS ALONE.
MANGA CLUB
THERE SHE IS...
DOZE...

FWMP
MIGHT AS WELL BE HER BEDROOM AT THIS POINT.
skrt
skrt
skrt
FWUP
!

OH.
GOOD MORNING, SENPAI.
MM...
GOTTA PEE.
sway sway
That looks unsafe.
HUP...
SHWF
HNNPH ...
GAAAH!! DON'T DO IT THEEERE!!

MNYA... MNYA...
THAT'S NOT A TOILET!
UGH, YOU'RE STILL HALF-ASLEEP!
GRRR!
WHAT-EVER! QUIT USING THE CLUBROOM AS YOUR BEDROOM!
I'M NOT *THAT* SLEEPY.
IT WAS OBVIOUSLY A JOKE.
SHWP
SHE'S NOT A CLUB MEMBER.
NO, THIS IS SAWADA, ONE GRADE BELOW ME.
BUT IT'S ALL DARK AND GLOOMY. PERFECT FOR SLEEPING!
ALL SHE DOES IS SLEEP.
GEE, SORRY IT'S SO GLOOMY...
Y'KNOW I DIDN'T MEAN IT LIKE THAT.
THE ONE TIME I PASSED BY HER CLASS...
SHE WAS DEAD ASLEEP ON HER DESK.
WHETHER CLASS IS IN SESSION OR NOT, I HEAR SHE SLEEPS THROUGH IT ALL.

SOMETIMES SHE SKIPS CLASS TO SLEEP IN VARIOUS SPOTS AROUND SCHOOL.
FOR WHATEVER REASON, SHE LIKES THIS CLUBROOM BEST AND WON'T LEAVE.
HOW LONG'VE YOU BEEN HERE?
HMM, I'VE BEEN ASLEEP FOR TWO, THREE HOURS, I THINK.
SAWADA, YOU'RE GONNA GET HELD BACK.
I DON'T CARE.
WON'T THE SCHOOL EVENTUALLY FORCE YOU TO DROP OUT?
......
OKAY, BUT LIKE...
WHY DO YOU JUST SLEEP THROUGH EVERYTHING ANYWAY?
...
WHY...

WOULD I STAY AWAKE IN THIS STUPID WORLD?
GLUB...
GLUB.

GA-K'RSH
JOLT
JOLT
JOLT
JOLT
THRSH
THRSH
THRSH
ONE DAY, SHE LASHED OUT. SHE STOPPED COMING TO SCHOOL AFTER THAT.

RUMOR WAS SHE DID STUFF LIKE THAT REGU-LARLY.
......
glance...
......
AT LEAST NOW I CAN MAKE SOME PROGRESS ON MY SKETCHES.
IT'S WEIRD HOW QUIET IT IS...
WITHOUT THE SOUND OF HER SLEEPY BREATHING.

ONE WEEK LATER.
GA-CHAK.
NO SIGN OF HER...
KLATTA...
MANGA CLUB
GA-CHAK
OH.
THERE YOU ARE...
SENPAI.

SAWADA ...
HOW...
HAVE YOU BEEN?

I'VE BEEN OKAY.
I-I SEE...
UHH... IF YOU DON'T MIND ME ASKING...
WHAT HAPPENED TO YOU?
YOU KNOW HOW PEOPLE SOMETIMES TOSS THEIR TRASH IN OTHER PEOPLE'S BIKE BASKETS?
HUH?
IT HAPPENS TO ME PRETTY OFTEN.
LIKE YESTERDAY, WHEN I WENT TO THE BOOKSTORE.
I CAME OUT, AND THERE WAS A JUICE CAN IN THE BASKET.
AND IT WAS STILL MORE THAN HALF-FULL.

I COULDN'T JUST LEAVE IT THERE, SO I TOOK IT HOME TO GET RID OF IT.
BUT I COULDN'T GET OVER THE FACT THAT SOMEONE HAD DONE THAT...
SO I SPENT THE REST OF THE DAY BIKING ALL OVER TOWN.
AND THEN ...
I WAS SO DEAD TIRED AND UNSTEADY ...
THAT I FELL RIGHT OFF A CLIFF.
AND HERE I AM NOW!
Tee hee!

!
TUG
SERI-OUSLY?!
TUG
SHAWAH-DAH?
SHA...
STRE-
EETCH
IT QUICKLY GETS TO BE TOO MUCH.
THE SECOND YOU STEP OUT-SIDE, IT'S ALL INCONSIDERATE JACKASSES LIKE THAT...

TELL ME!!
DWUMP
WHAT AM I SUPPOSED TO DO ABOUT IT?!

WELL, THIS IS HOW I DEAL WITH IT.
ANYTIME I STEP OUTSIDE MY HOUSE...
I THINK OF THE WORLD LIKE AN RPG.
ONCE YOU LEAVE THE SAFETY OF YOUR VILLAGE...
THERE'S ALL SORTS OF MONSTERS OUT THERE.

OR THE KIND OF MONSTER THAT LEAVES GARBAGE IN ANOTHER PERSON'S BIKE BASKET.
WHETHER IT'S AN OUT-OF-CONTROL OLD DUDE, DELINQUENT BRATS ON LOUD BIKES...
SOMEONE STEALING UMBRELLAS FROM A RACK...
Y'SEE, I ONCE CHASED AFTER SOMEONE WHO STOLE MY UMBRELLA, AND I ASKED THEM...
"WHY WOULD YOU DO THAT?"

AND THEY SAID TO ME...
"HUH?
"CHEAP, PLASTIC UMBRELLAS ARE BASICALLY COMMUNITY PROPERTY, RIGHT?
"ONE OF THOSE 'LET'S ALL SHARE' KIND OF THINGS.
"YOU GET ME?"
I REALIZED THEY WERE BEYOND HELP.
THEY WERE A MON-STER.
WHEN I THINK OF IT LIKE THAT...
IT'S EASIER TO ACCEPT REALITY.
HUNH...
I SEE. MONSTERS. HUNH...

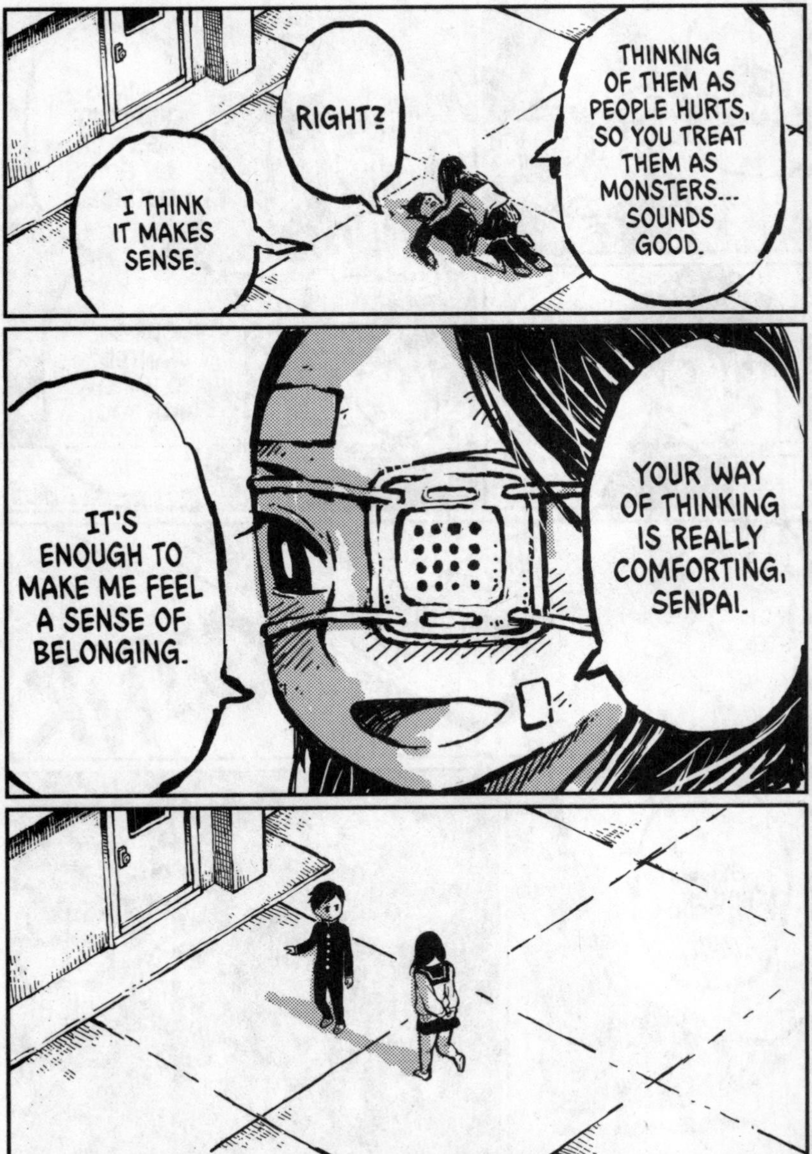
THINKING OF THEM AS PEOPLE HURTS, SO YOU TREAT THEM AS MONSTERS... SOUNDS GOOD.
RIGHT?
I THINK IT MAKES SENSE.
YOUR WAY OF THINKING IS REALLY COMFORTING, SENPAI.
IT'S ENOUGH TO MAKE ME FEEL A SENSE OF BELONGING.

I WAS READY TO GIVE UP ON GOING OUTSIDE...
BUT I WANTED TO HANG WITH YOU.
I'M GLAD I CAME.
THAT'S GOOD.
GTNK
STILL, THOUGH...

I KINDA WISH THE WORLD COULD GET A FRESH START.

WITH JUST THE TWO OF US LEFT OVER.

WHAT WOULD WE DO BY OUR- SELVES?
I'D JUST MESS WITH YOU FOR FUN!
OH, GEE, THANKS. SOUNDS GREAT.
sway...
OH...
NO...
sway...
Sway...
I FEEL SO... TIRED...
H-HEY!! SAWADA!!
DMP DMP
S- SENPAI...
I'M SORRY...
BUT COULD YOU HELP ME GET HOME?

THIS IT?
Y-YEAH. THANKS SO MUCH...
NOBODY ELSE HOME?
NOPE...
MY MOM... IS AT WORK...
IT'S JUST... THE TWO OF...
US...
UH, SAWADA?
SUU SUU

SUU SUU
SKRTCH
SKRTCH
SUU SUU

......
SUU
SUU
I'M REALLY MAKING PROGRESS.
HALT
THE SOUND OF HER BREATHING WHILE SHE SLEEPS IS COMFORTING. HUNH...
AND WITH THAT, I FINISHED THE ROUGH DRAFT...
WITCH ROMI
OF THE NEXT WORK I'D PUT IN THE CLUB NEWSLETTER.

WITH SAWADA'S BREATHING AS BACK-GROUND NOISE.
SUU
SUU
SUU
A ROUGH DRAFT CREATED ...
I'M A WITCH!
HEE HEE!
SO THAT MONSTER WAS YOUR DOING?
YUP, THAT'S RIGHT.
IT STARTED AS A MONSTER-FIGHTING FANTASY, BUT CHANGED TO A STORY ABOUT A MONSTER-MAKING WITCH AND HER INTERACTIONS WITH THE LEAD.
HOLD ON... IS THIS WITCH ME?
I DIDN'T INTENTIONALLY MODEL HER AFTER YOU, BUT SEEMS IT SORTA WENT THAT WAY.
BUT IN THIS STORY, I CREATE MONSTERS ...
THAT MAKES ME THE VIL-LAIN!

NO, NO, THAT WASN'T MY INTENT!
THE MONSTERS IN THIS STORY ARE LIKE AN ABSTRACT REPRESENTATION...
UHHH... THIS IS SO HARD TO EXPLAIN...
LIKE, THE POINT OF MANGA IS TO SHOW IDEAS THAT'RE TOUGH TO EXPLAIN WITH WORDS ALONE.
......
YOU REMEMBER OUR DISCUSSION ABOUT THINKING OF THE PEOPLE YOU HATE AS MONSTERS?
OF COURSE I REMEMBER!
THAT'S WHY I DON'T LIKE THIS!
WHY AM *I* CREATING THE PEOPLE I HATE...THESE MONSTERS?!
N-NO! THE MONSTERS THAT THIS WITCH CREATES...
AREN'T THE ONES THAT REPRESENT THE PEOPLE YOU HATE!

LOOK, AFTER I TOLD YOU ABOUT MY WORLD-VIEW...
I THOUGHT LONG AND HARD ABOUT CALLING THEM "MONSTERS."
I REALIZED THAT COMPARING THE PEOPLE YOU HATE TO MONSTERS...
IS KINDA RUDE TO MONSTERS.
THAT MIGHT BE PARTLY 'CAUSE I LOVE MONSTERS IN CREATIVE WORKS.
BUT EVEN THOUGH MONSTERS HAVE CROOKED LOOKS AND SAVAGE PERSONALITIES...
I THINK THEY'RE REALLY BEAUTIFUL AND SENSITIVE CREATURES.
SO, I DON'T WANNA USE MONSTERS...
TO REFER TO THE PEOPLE THAT YOU OR I HATE.
THOSE PEOPLE... THEY...
HAVE SUCH MEAN LOOKS...
......
I'M NOT TOTALLY SOLD...
BUT I UNDERSTAND A BIT BETTER NOW.

MONSTERS ARE HONEST IN APPEAR- ANCE.
PEOPLE WHOSE PER- SONALITIES AND APPEARANCES DON'T SYNC ARE THE REAL TWISTED ONES.
OKAY, LET'S THINK OF A NEW NAME FOR THE TWISTED PEOPLE.
......
YOU'RE RIGHT. IT'S RUDE TO PUT THEM IN THE SAME BOX.
SOUNDS SIMILAR TO "HUMANS," BUT WHEN YOU SAY IT...
REMEMBER TO ADD THE "EWW" IN YOUR HEAD!
HA HA HA!
WILL DO! I LIKE THAT!
SEEING AS NOTHING'S COMING TO MIND...
LET'S CALL THEM "HEWW- MANS" FOR NOW.
HMM ...
HMM ...
......
......

I STARTED CLEANING UP THE ROUGH DRAFT FOR PRINT...
AND COULDN'T GET A THING DONE WITHOUT THE SOUND OF SAWADA'S BREATHING...
SO I WAS ONLY ABLE TO WORK ON IT AFTER SCHOOL IN THE CLUBROOM.
SAWADA WAS COMING TO SCHOOL AGAIN BUT STILL AVOIDED CLASS.
SHE SLEPT AWAY THE DAYS IN THE CLUBROOM, NEVER GOING HOME EITHER.
I WAS KINDA THANKFUL.
I GOT TONS OF WORK DONE...
AND EVENTUALLY, I STOPPED GOING TO MY CLASSES, TOO.
I DIDN'T GO HOME...
ALL DAY, EVERY DAY, I WORKED ON MY MANGA.

SUU
SUU
skritch
skritch
skritch
SUU
SUU
SUU
SUU
SUU
PLP
INK

plip...
INK
FOR ART

SUU
SUU
SUU
NYU

F...
FINALLY ...
IT'S DONE.
I CAN'T REMEMBER THE LAST TIME I COMPLETED A STORY LIKE THIS.
COULDN'T HAVE DONE IT WITHOUT YOU, SAWA--

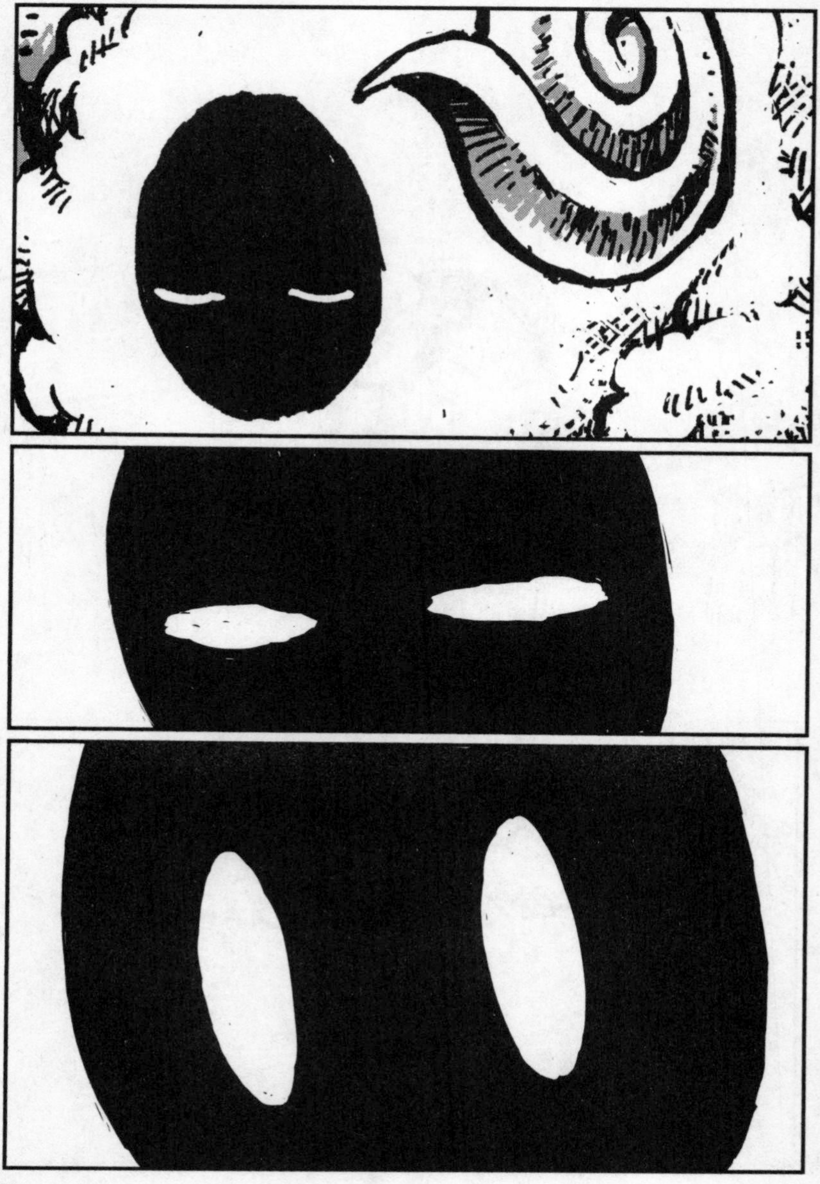

Episode 11: Recollection | End

Episode 12

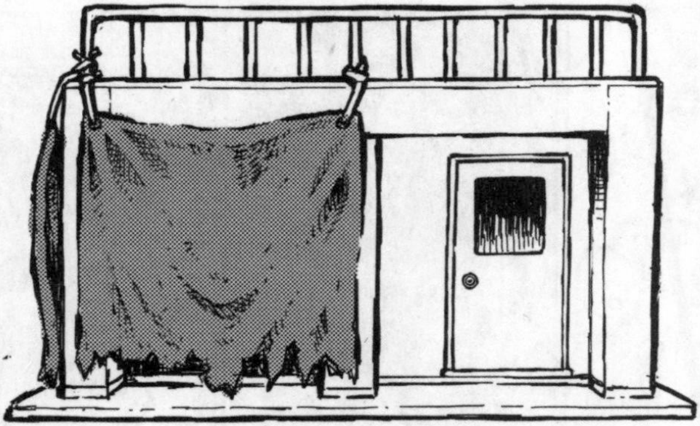

An Important Place

WAKE UP...
SENPAI, WAKE UP.
JOLT
HWUH?!!
WE'RE AT THE SCHOOL.
OH...
HUH? WAS I SLEEPING?
YES, THE WHOLE WAY HERE.
GOT-CHA...
THAT DREAM... WOW...
NOW I REMEMBER...
......
GA-CHAK
GA-CHAK

......
KNCH
KNCH
THE...THE SCHOOL REALLY DID DIE!
NO, NOT REALLY.
IT HAS TO BE OUR SCHOOL.
L-LET'S JUST FIND A NEW HOME!
THEN WE CAN PUT UP A BARRIER AND LIVE THERE... RIGHT?
TP TP
THAT'S WHY I MADE SURE TO PROTECT IT UNTIL THE VERY END.
DOESN'T EXIST WITHOUT A SCHOOL.
OUR WHOLE SENPAI/ KOUHAI RELATION-SHIP...

SLIDE
AT SCHOOL, I COULD SEE YOU.
THAT WAS ITS ONE SAVING GRACE.
ALL I HAD TO DO WAS GO TO SCHOOL...
AND WITH YOU AS MY SENPAI, I COULD BE WITH YOU, NO EXCUSES NEEDED.
BUT...

IF THE SCHOOL SUDDENLY DISAP-PEARED...
AND WE, TWO PEOPLE WITH NO RELATION TO EACH OTHER...
WERE THROWN INTO SOME HUGE SPACE WITH A BUNCH OF PEOPLE...
TOSS
TOSS
I WOULDN'T BE ABLE TO CALL OUT TO YOU...
OR BE AROUND YOU.
WITHOUT A SPECIFIC SYSTEM OR MY ARMOR AS YOUR "KOUHAI"...
I WOULD BE TOO AFRAID TO APPROACH YOU.

I'M SUCH A DIFFICULT PERSON.
I KNOW THAT.
I KNOW, BUT I STILL CAN'T HELP IT...
EVEN WITHOUT THE SCHOOL OR WHATEVER, YOU AND I ARE STILL JUST THAT!
YOU DON'T HAVE TO WORRY ABOUT THAT!
TAK
THE WHITE MIASMA INSIDE ME IS UNBELIEVABLY FRAGILE.
IT'S EASILY OVER-WHELMED BY THE BLACK.
SO...
I INTENDED TO HAVE FUN LIVING WITH YOU HERE AT SCHOOL...
UNTIL THE MOMENT THAT THIS WORLD AND I WERE CONSUMED BY THE BLACK MIASMA.
fwp
TAK
TAK
fwp

I...
I'M SORRY... I WAS SO INSISTENT ABOUT EXPLORING THE OUTSIDE WORLD...
CLENCH...
PLEASE DON'T WORRY ABOUT THAT. I'M GLAD WE WENT.
IT WAS A LOT OF FUN EXPLORING WITH YOU, SENPAI.
BUT UNFORTUNATELY...
fwp
TAK
THE LOSS OF THE SCHOOL...
THE SAFE HARBOR OF OUR RELATIONSHIP...
fwp
TAK...
BROUGHT WITH IT A HUGE AND UNCONTROLLABLE AMOUNT OF DESPAIR.

JSHH...
WE DIDN'T GET TO SPEND MUCH TIME IN OUR OWN LITTLE WORLD HERE...BUT IT WAS REALLY FUN.
SENPAI...

GANK
HUH...?
SA...
SAWADA...?

!!
KLAK
KLAK

TAK
TAK
TAK
TAK
TAK
TAK
TAK
TAK
TAK
TAK
TAK
TAK

AAH...
AH...
ZURU...
GA-TAK
BWSH
HYUU
SHOON

WH- WHAT'S GOING ON?
IT...IT'S GOTTA BE A NIGHT- MARE...
SEN... PAI...
THIS IS... WHAT I WANTED... TO GIVE YOU...

ZLORCH
ZLUP
ZU ZU...
HERE...
IT'S VERY IMPORTANT TO ME, SO I ISOLATED IT WITHIN MYSELF...
I COATED IT... WITH ALL THE WHITE MIASMA I HAD LEFT...

THE MANGA CLUB'S...
ROOM...?

SAWADA!!
IN A FEW SECONDS, THE WORLD...WILL BE CONSUMED...BY THE BLACK MIASMA.
WHEN THAT HAPPENS, I THINK...
THE WORLD YOU KNEW WILL CHANGE ONCE AGAIN.
THE CLUBROOM IS SAFE FOR NOW, SO PLEASE TAKE SHELTER...

GRIP
H-HOLD ON A SEC!!
I REMEMBERED WHAT HAPPENED!!
THIS... THIS IS ALL MY FAULT, ISN'T IT?!!
IT'S BECAUSE OF THAT MANGA I DREW!!
NO, SENPAI...
THE BLACK MIASMA...
AND THE MONSTERS... THEY'RE ALL PIECES OF ME...
SO...
PWOK

ホ BWOOF ン
MANGA CLUB
!!
DUN
WHEN YOU VENTURE BACK OUT AFTER THE MIASMA DISSIPATES...
KR
SENPAI...

KRII...
PLEASE FIND ALL THE LITTLE PIECES OF ME AND...
KR-III...

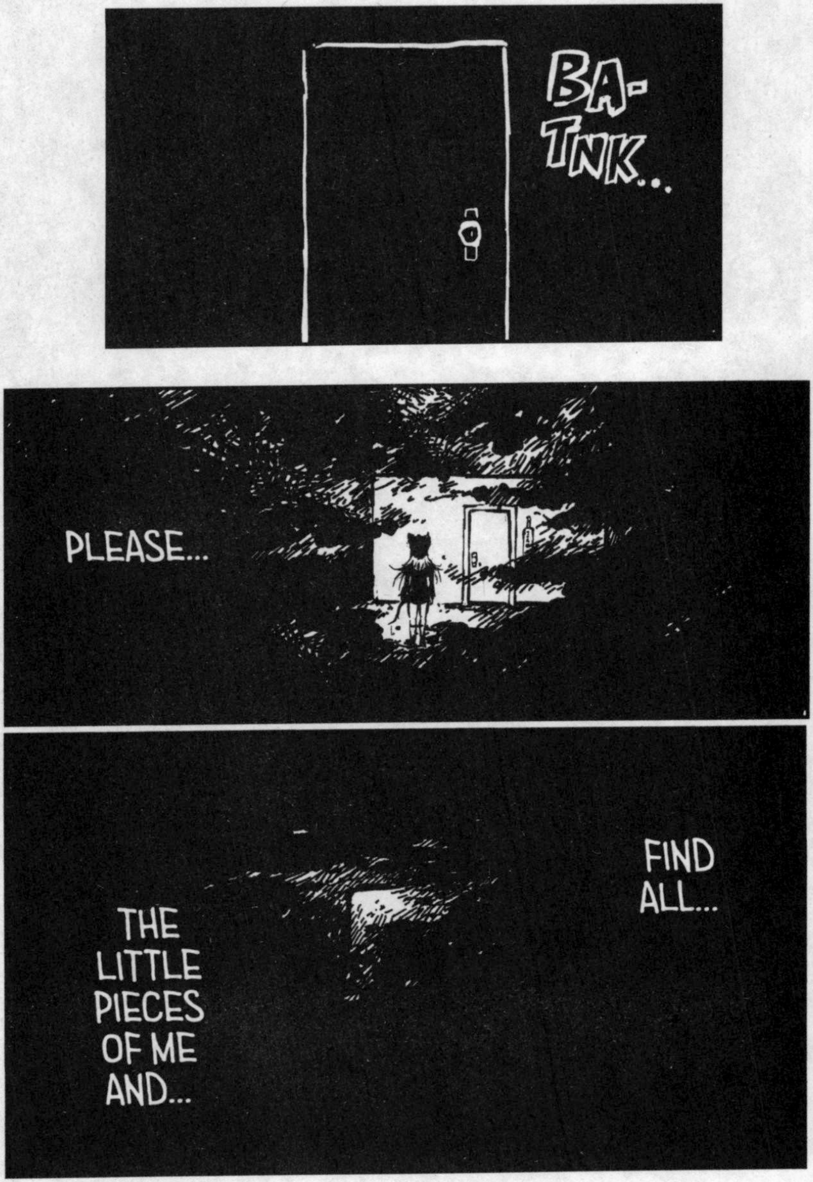
BA-TNK...
PLEASE...
FIND ALL...
THE LITTLE PIECES OF ME AND...

BREAK
THEM.

Episode 12:
An Important Place | End